Sewing for Guinea Pigs

13 Sewing Projects for Your Cavy

By Danielle Pientka

Copyright © 2019 by Danielle Pientka

All rights reserved.

Table of Contents

Introduction 3

Cage Liners 5

Wet Bag 15

Cleaning Wipes and Cleaner 19

Fleece Forest 23

Tunnel 31

Cuddle Cave 37

Cube House 42

Hay Sack 56

Ball Toy 62

Corner Hammock 65

Snuffle Mat 69

Lap Blanket 74

Ladder Cover 79

Conclusion 86

Glossary 87

About the Author 91

Introduction

Your guinea pigs are part of the family. You spend time snuggling them, a lot of time cleaning up after them, and you provide them with treats and love.

Guinea pigs live 4-8 years with proper care. They're affectionate and will 'wheek' to say 'hello' when they hear you, particularly if you are **the giver of all good treats** (mine love lettuce!).

You'll be seeing a lot of their cage. The cage needs to be large, which means using a lot of paper bedding if you go that route. We decided to go with ecofriendly fabric cage liners to save money. I love reusable products and the bedding is fluffy and soft.

But the liners are just a gateway to all of the other fun things you can create for the cage. There are hay bags and hammocks, and they can all be made in matching sets. Imagine making a set for Christmas, a set for Valentine's and other holidays! It's so much fun to pick out cute fabrics for their cage.

I hope this book helps teach you how to spoil your guinea pigs with custom products fit to your cage.

Happy sewing!

Cage Liners

These are a great project to start with because they're simple rectangles, use a lot of upcycled fabric (if you want to upcycle to save money), and they're useful.

First, let me talk a little about the cage liners that I make. I use a layer of Polyurethane Laminate (PUL) for the bottom or you could use fleece that is non wicking. In the middle, I add an absorbency layer from upcycled prefold diapers or old towels. The top needs to be a stay dry layer: prepped wicking fleece, alova suedecloth, and microfleece are viable options for that.

Please see the glossary for more information on some of these fabric choices.

Left: Fleece top, Right: Alova Suedecloth top. The brown

fabric on top is Microfleece

If you don't want to pick up PUL, which can be expensive, or alova suedecloth/microfleece, which is difficult to find, you could use a wicking fleece for the top and non-wicking fleece for the bottom. I have made quite a few like that as well. They're super cozy.

Some people choose the no sew option and layer fabric in the cage so they can swap out the absorbency fabric. I sew my layers together. I prefer it because it makes the entire liner heavier than if they were laid out separately. This makes it harder for the guinea pig to lift up or shift. It also makes the liner easy to fold and store when not in use.

Supplies

- Size 14 universal needle (this will help to sew through the thick layers with ease)
- PUL or some type of laminated fabric with the laminated portion facing up. Alternatively you can use a non-wicking fleece.
- Prefolds, towels, or something that will absorb water or urine for the middle.
- Stay-dry fabric such as fleece (prepped), microfleece, or alova suedecloth

Instructions

You need to measure the size of your cage or the section of the cage that you're sewing your liner for. I sewed a liner for the small part of my cage and one for the large part. The small area has food and water in it so it will need more frequent changes. It was cheaper and easier to make five to seven small liners and two big liners than it was to make a bunch of big liners for the entire cage. I also find smaller liners easier to sew and wash than extra-large.

Once you get your measurements, add ½" seam allowance to each side. This means my liners, 35x24" and 12x24" finished, were made from fabric cut to 36x25" and 13x25."

You'll need one cut of PUL, one cut for your absorbency layer, and one cut for your stay dry layer. You can cut your absorbency layer slightly smaller if you want to make sewing the edges easier- this is particularly helpful if your sewing machine can't handle thick layers.

Old polyurethane laminate fabric. The "soft" top is a normal fabric with the bottom (the ugly side) being laminated to make it waterproof (ish).

If you're upcycling towels or prefolds, you will want to sew them together so they're the correct size. I patched together everything for my liners to save money. It was more time consuming, but I was pleased to use scraps.

If you're new to sewing, just use a large towel for the absorbency because it will simplify the process a bit.

This looks like a whole lot of craziness, but you could make this easier by just using a towel for the absorbency or a large cut of absorbency fabric.

You can now sew the absorbency layer to the PUL, shiny side up with the absorbency on top. I usually sew a few straight lines from one end to the other to hold the absorbency and the PUL together. This just helps keep everything from shifting around in the wash.

Now place your soft side of the PUL right sides together with your stay dry layer. Your sewing machine will be sewing through pretty thick layers if you're using something like prefolds, so make sure to use a good needle that can accommodate it.

Sew right sides together, leaving an area the size of your fist to turn the fabric right sides out.

Turn right sides out.

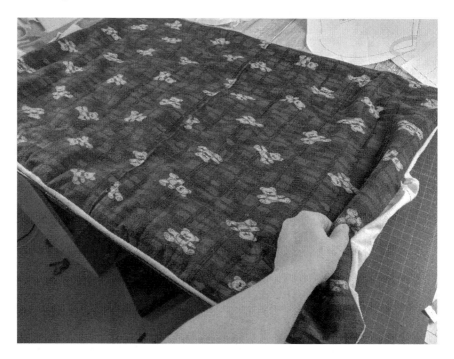

Fold the edges from the opening under, and top stitch.

You're done!

How to Clean the Cage

Wondering how to clean the cage when you have liners? It's pretty easy. You lay the liners in the cage. Each day, you can shake the poop off the liners into a container or the toilet. Alternatively, you could use a small dustbin and brush to sweep them up or you could get a small hand vacuum for this purpose. Either way, you ditch the hard poops.

I use a small liner in the area for the food and water zone- this area gets more build up and as a result, the liner needs to be changed more frequently. That liner is changed daily. You can use a bucket or wet bag to store the dirty liners. The larger liner seems to be fine to only change once or twice a week. I wanted seven small liners and two large liners so I would always have a full load of guinea pig laundry to do together without needed to use an alternative bedding while the wash was run.

There were a couple areas that I still needed to do spot cleanings on with a vinegar and water mix. One was the ladder area because that didn't have a liner over it, and the other area was a spot along the side where the liner turned up, but overall you can see that the liners otherwise did a great job.

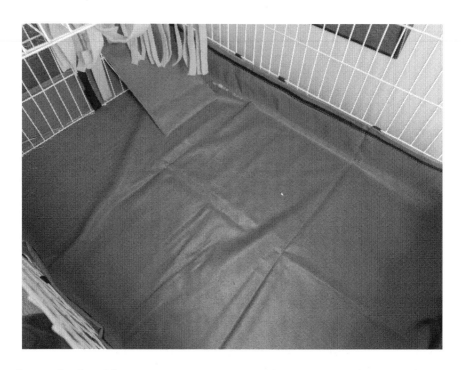

Laundering Liners

These liners can be laundered on high heat if needed. Do not use fabric softener or any detergent that has fabric softener because you will ruin the absorbency of your liners. You can search for "cloth diaper safe laundry detergent" if needed, but usually free and clear type products work well.

For cloth diapers, I usually run a rinse cycle on cold, then follow up with a heavy cycle on hot. I haven't been doing the pre-rinse with these, but I may change that if I notice any ammonia smell.

You want to make sure to shake any poop or hay off the liners before you put them in the wash.

Why Liners?

While paper bedding is compostable and an ecofriendly option for your guinea pig cage, I thought it was really messy and harder to keep clean. I also assume it gets expensive long term to keep buying more of it, and making it doesn't appear to be a viable option.

Reusable liners cost more upfront, but you can save money by sewing your own and you'll be able to use them until they wear out. With proper care, and assuming your cavies don't eat them, you could get a few years or more of use out of these.

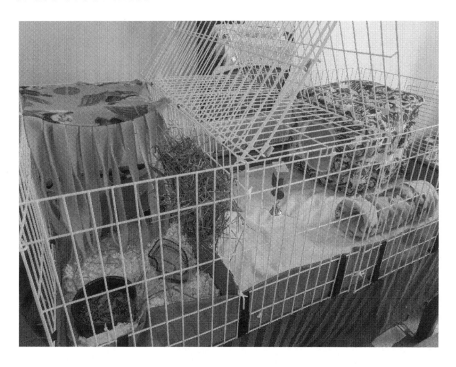

Figure 1: Cage liner pictured on the right, paper bedding

on the left.

Wet Bag

This isn't a new item for us. We own wet bags for cloth diapers and we use them in the kitchen for dish cloths. Whenever you're using reusable items like cage liners, it's nice to have somewhere to store the dirty liners until you have enough to do a load of laundry.

The nice thing about these bags is that they can be washed with your liners if needed.

With my cloth diapers, I add a zipper to keep it closed, but I make the wet bag for the guinea pig liners slightly different. The zipper mostly helps keeps the smell in, but the guinea pig area is going to have an odor regardless, so I didn't stress with adding a zipper. Instead I made it easy to shove liners in and large enough to hold one load of guinea pig laundry.

The photo above is actually my kitchen wet bag, but it's a great size for cage liners as well.

Supplies

- PUL or some type of laminated fabric with the laminated portion facing up.
- Snaps and snap pliers

Instructions

You want to start by cutting your fabric. In the wet bag pictured, I actually sewed together lots of piece of scrap PUL to create the bag. You only need two large pieces, however, if you have full size PUL.

Cut two large pieces of PUL that are 18" W x 27" T. You'll also want to cut (4) 2x11" pieces for the straps.

Lay the two large pieces of PUL right sides together. Sew along two long sides and one short side, in a U shape. Keep in mind that the side you aren't sewing is the top so make sure the fabric design faces in the correct direction.

Now you need to finish the top of your bag. Fold over the edge once (or twice if you want the raw edge completely hidden). Sew a straight stitch around.

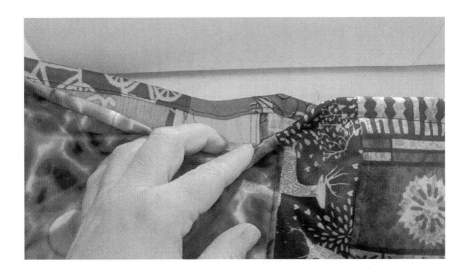

You'll want to sew your straps now. Take two of your strips and face them right sides together. Sew both long sides and one short side. Turn right sides out. Turn the edges under on the open end then top stitch the whole strap.

Repeat with your second strap.

Use a straight stitch to sew one end of each strap to either side of the back of the wet bag. I like to sew a square/rectangle with an X through it.

While you could certainly sew down the other end of the strap too so the strap forms a closed loop, I prefer to add snaps so I can open and close the strap. This allows me to snap the wet bag over a towel bar or the like.

Add your snaps to each strap.

Need more information on using snap pliers? Check out https://diydanielle.com/how-to-use-snaps-and-snap-pliers/

Cleaning Wipes and Cleaner

You'll want to keep some cleaner and wipes beside your cage for cleaning. It's nice to be able to wipe out the cage bottom as needed. Generally, my thick liners do a good job at preventing pee from soaking through to the bottom of the cage, but you still want to wipe the bottom occasionally and clean up any spots that sneak through.

While you could use a chemical cleaner and a paper towel, I prefer to use a cloth wipe or rag because I'm already doing the laundry anyways and it is nice to save money on disposables.

Tip: I usually use a bit of baking soda in the bottom of my guinea pig litter box to help cut down on smells. I use paper bedding in the litter box area only.

Supplies

- Flannel
- An empty glass bottle
- Vinegar
- Water

Instructions for the Cleaner

The cleaner is simple to make. I love to use vinegar when I clean, and you can even pick up cleaning vinegar which is stronger than the stuff you cook with. Ammonia and bleach are both a bit touchy for using around animals so it's better to avoid them for the safety of your guinea pigs.

Take an old spray bottle and clean it out thoroughly. I run water through the sprayer repeatedly until any smells from the previous product is gone.

Once that's done, I simply mix vinegar and water together. How much you mix will depend on if you use cleaning vinegar or regular vinegar. For regular vinegar, I mix 50-50 water and vinegar. Please read the instructions on your container of cleaning vinegar if you choose to use that.

Shake. Spray and wipe down where needed.

Instructions for the Wipes

Your wipes for cleaning can be as simple as cut up rags. If you want to make rags, cut old tee-shirts or towels into squares to use to wipe things up. T-shirts won't fray so you can use as is, but if you cut up towels then you'll want to finish the edges with your sewing machine or serger to keep them from fraying.

Generally, I make my wipes out of flannel though. It's often on sale and it's one of the more affordable fabric options. You can make "one ply" wipes (with one piece of flannel), but I prefer a thicker wipe, so I use two layers.

8"x8" is a good size to use for a cleaning wipe. Take your flannel and cut up (2) 8x8 pieces of flannel per wipe that you need to make. I've found that one per day is more than enough.

Face two cuts of flannel right sides together. Sew a straight stitch around the fabric, stopping about 1.5-2" from where you started. You will flip your fabric right sides out through that small gap.

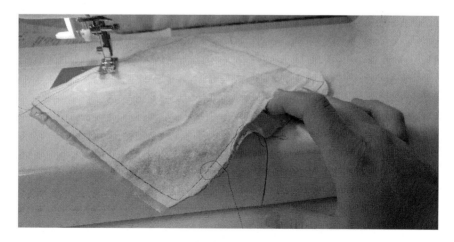

The corners generally get stuck a bit when turning the

fabric right sides out, so I use a chopstick or another thin item to poke the corners out.

You should now use your iron to press the fabric flat. Tuck under the open portion and iron that flat.

Now you should use a straight stitch to top stitch the fabric. This will close up your 1.5-2" gap and leave you with a finished wipe.

Repeat for your other wipes!

Next time you clean your cage, you can spray the vinegar and water mixture on your cage floor then clean it up with your new wipes.

Fleece Forest

My guinea pigs love their fleece forest and it's a pretty easy project. You could do this as a no sew project pretty easily, but I wanted a finished look so I did the extra work.

Supplies

- Fleece
- Eyelets or grommets (an alternative would be to sew on straps that you can tie onto the cage)
- Clips or zip ties to hold them on. I think clips would be a nice option so you could move it around the cage.
- Scissors

Instructions

This is a pretty easy project, although I am going to suggest an easier way. I probably spent a bit too much time on this.

You want to work with fleece for this because it's nonfraying.

Start by cutting two squares of fabric that are each 12x12". These measurements came from my cage setup so you may want to adjust yours. The train fabric is for my top and the green fabric is for the bottom part of my fleece forest.

After cutting my squares, I cut a bunch of long strips of fleece. You want these to be long enough to reach the floor of your cage from the top of the fleece forest (or thereabouts). You could do all different lengths if you want.

I cut enough for two sides of my fleece forest. I decided to not add them to the other two sides.

I also took a piece of fabric and cut strips in it, leaving a small strip at the top uncut. This part was to sew across the bottom of the forest (versus along the sides).

Sew this strip straight across the middle of the bottom square for your fleece forest.

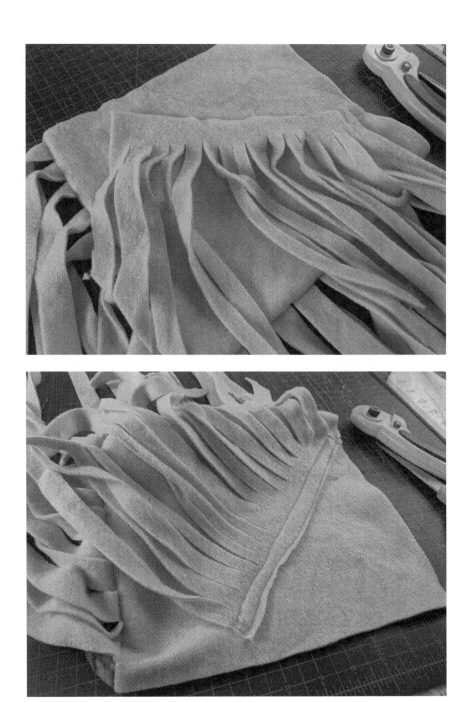

At this point you want to place your top square right sides up and your bottom square right sides down. Your fleece strips are sandwiched between the two fabrics along the two sides you want the strips to hang down (you can add strips on all four sides if you prefer). My strands were long, so I needed to tuck them into the middle.

Once you've done this and pinned, go ahead and stitch around the whole piece, leaving a small area to turn it right sides out.

Turn it right sides out, then top stitch it.

Now I just added eyelets (grommets) to each corner to hang the fleece forest from the top of the cage.

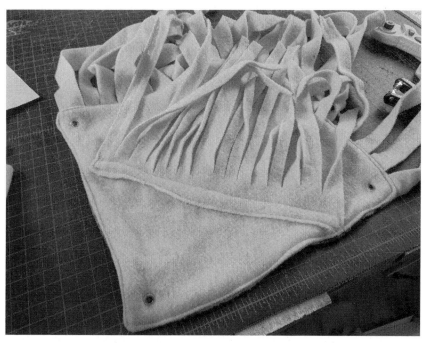

I used zip ties to hold them on the cage initially but I decided to replace those with binder rings so it would be easier to move the fleece forest around if I wanted.

The guinea pigs love it. It's a fun place for them to hide and I think they like to use that area when going to the bathroom so if you're potty training, you may want to consider adding a litter box to that zone of the cage. Guinea pigs often feel safer using the bathroom or eating where they have some type of cover, given that they're prey animals.

Tunnel

Tunnels are a lot of fun and give your cavy another place to hide. They love being able to run from one hidey-hole to another in their cage. The challenge to explaining this project to you is that the sizing will vary depending on the size of your guinea pigs. I have Abyssinian guinea pigs which, I believe, are a bit smaller than some other breeds. My first tunnel was super tiny and fit them as babies. Since then, I have made two others that fit them at other stages.

Plan to adjust your size as needed. My final tunnel (as my guinea pigs are full size now) was made with a cut of fabric 22" W and 17" Length.

Supplies

- Fleece
- Optional: Dritz Featherlite Boning, 2-Yard

Instructions

You'll need to start by determining how large you need your tunnel to be. If you can find a container that your guinea pigs fit through easily, you can take those measurements and add a seam allowance to your fabric.

For my largest guinea pig tunnel, I cut my fleece fabric 22x17. The 22" is what is going around them so you can figure out if your guinea pig will fit if you take your measuring tape and see if they are fatter or thinner than 22" around (really 21" with seam allowance accounted for).

The 17" is the length of the tunnel, subtracting a seam allowance and the amount you roll over at each end.

You need to cut an interior and exterior piece of fleece for these measurements.

Once you cut your fleece, you need to fold each piece in half right sides together so the 22" is 11". Sew a straight stitch along the long edge (in the picture below I used a serger for the edge, but a straight stitch will be fine).

Once you do this, you should have 2 tunnel shapes.

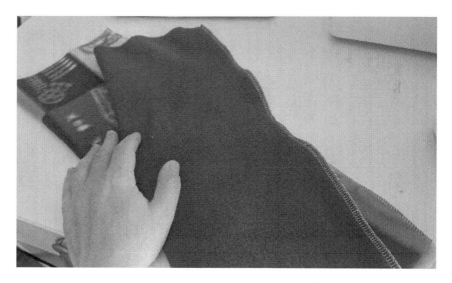

The exterior fabric tunnel should be turned right sides out and you can tuck the interior fabric into the exterior tunnel piece. Line everything up.

Fleece does not fray so I didn't bother trying to hide the raw edges. I just sewed a straight stitch around each end to combine the inner and outer tunnel pieces.

Once you've done this, you can turn your ends over once or twice. For my first two tunnels, I folded them over twice then sewed a straight stitch around. It hides the raw edge and the bulk of the fabric helps keep the ends open.

For my third tunnel, I decided to add the boning. I think over time the tunnel flattens without it because the guinea pigs trample it. The boning should prevent this.

To add it, I turn the edges over and sewed around the opening, creating what is called a **casing**. You leave a small opening to feed your boning through. Attaching a safety pin to the end of your boning helps make it easier to pull through the casing.

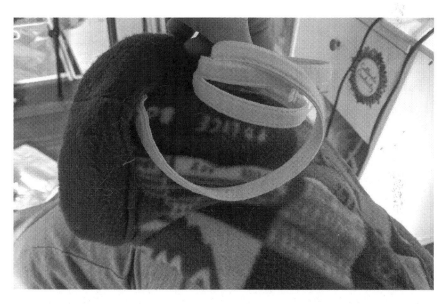

Once you get to the other side, you can cut the boning to size and sew the two ends of the boning together.

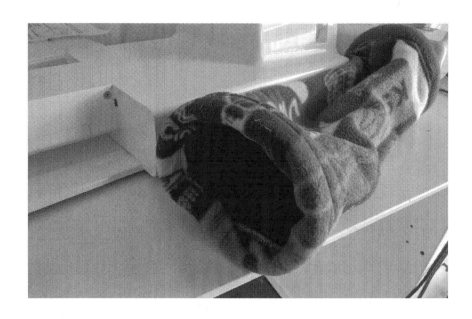

Cuddle Cave

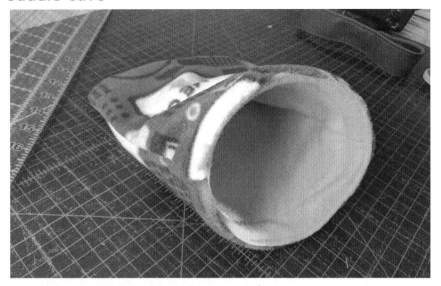

Cuddle caves are awesome to keep in the cage to give guinea pigs a nice cozy place to hide and snuggle, but they're also perfect for helping kids get comfortable with their guinea pigs. It's safer for the kids to hold the guinea pigs in a cuddle cave instead of their bare hands so they don't accidentally squeeze them too hard if the cavies try to sneak away.

I made one of these for each of my kids and they love them.

Supplies

- Fleece fabric: Interior and exterior cuts
- Dritz Featherlite Boning, 2-Yard

Instructions

Start by cutting out your interior and exterior fabric. You'll need fleece cut as following:

- (2) 14x10.5" pieces of the interior fabric
- (2) 14x10.5" pieces of the exterior fabric.

Face the two interior pieces right sides together and sew around in a U shape. Repeat with the two exterior fabrics.

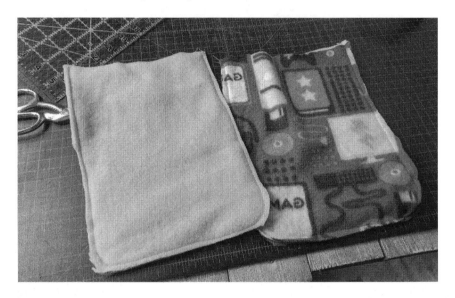

Flip your exterior fabric right sides out then tuck it into the interior fabric pieces. They should now be right sides together.

You'll now sew around the top, leaving a small space to turn the pieces right sides out.

When you're done, you will flip them right sides out through your gap. Like this photo below:

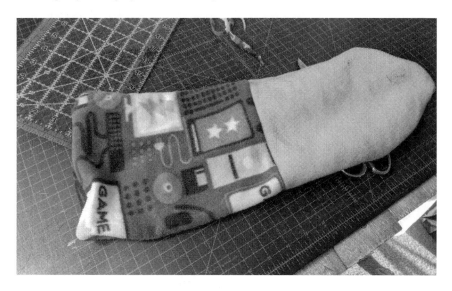

Now you can tuck the green into the gaming fabric.

At this point, you want to add your boning. The boning helps keep the opening open... otherwise, it will flop closed. This could be skipped because if you put the guinea pig in there, they'll snuffle it open when they want to come out. But if you plan to use it as a house in their cage, you'll want to use the boning so they can get back inside on their own.

Look at the width of your boning. You need to sew a line of stitches around the top of your bag so there is a casing slightly wider than the boning. This casing gives you a place to thread your boning through, so the boning doesn't shift all over your bag interior.

A safety pin clips to the fabric at the end of your boning allows you to feed the boning through the casing. Once you get it all the way around, cut your boning so that it's the right length for your cave opening. You can sew the fabric of each end of the boning together. This means snipping the boning itself a bit shorter than the white fabric surrounding it so your sewing needle doesn't hit the hard plastic.

Once your boning is connected, tuck it back into the casing. Now you need to top stitch the top of the bag so the gap you turned it through is sewn closed.

You're finished!

Cube House

I've made two of these cube houses and they're so much fun for the guinea pigs. They spend a lot of time in them and the house provides them with a place that feels safe and secure. These are big, but you can make them smaller if you prefer. I think using 10x10 squares would probably work for a smaller cube.

Supplies

- Fleece
- Bias tape
- Quilt Batting

Instructions

Cut your fabric:

- 6 pieces of fleece for the inside: 12x12"
- 6 pieces of fleece for the outside 12x12"
- 12 pieces of quilt batting 10x10"

I used two pieces of quilt batting each to add additional thickness and stability to the cube. I didn't want it to be floppy.

As you can probably see in the photos above, some of my quilt batting is just folded over 10x10 pieces (10x20 really). While I could cut separate 10x10 pieces and sew one to each inner piece and one to each outer piece, I decided to sew both pieces of batting to each inner piece.

If I did it again, I might sew the batting to the exterior fabric pieces instead and leave the inside pieces loosey-goosey. I'll discuss that a bit at the end.

The first thing I did was center my two pieces of batting on the inner fabric squares. The reason I choose to use the 10x10 size was to eliminate bulk around the seams., but it requires that you sew the batting to the fleece somehow. Sewing a few lines through both prevents the batting from bunching up and ensures that it stays put.

What shape or how you sew it on isn't super important. You could even do some pretty quilting if you wanted.

Do this to five pieces of fleece and 10 pieces of batting,

For the last inner fleece and two pieces of batting, you need to create your front panel where the entrance will be.

I found something circular in my sewing room and used it to create a template for a circle. This roll of packing tape worked.

Like the other five inner pieces with batting, you need to sew the batting on, centering it. Mine was messy looking but it'll do the trick.

For this step, you could place the outer fabric on and quilt all three pieces if you wanted. It would be easier to sew on the binding this way.

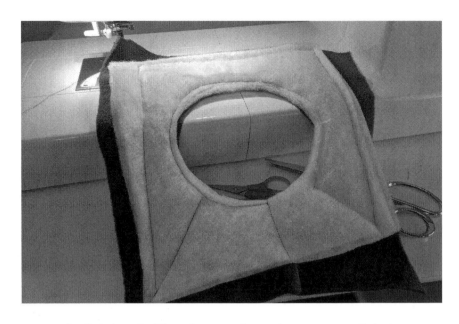

Instead of doing it like that, I pinned my outer fabric to the pieces seen above with the right sides out. Then I sewed binding around the circle.

A quick note on how I'm assembling it: You might be wondering why I won't assemble the front panel just like I'll be assembling the rest of the house. I THOUGHT about it. Ideally, I would do this and then not have any raw seams exposed anywhere. But fleece is forgiving with raw seams and if I did it that way, I'd need to sew on the binding AFTER the house was assembled. This is much more unwieldy in my opinion. So I chose the lesser of two evils.

I recommend using lots of pins to hold the binding in place, making sure to use a zig zag stitch to go over the binding as neatly as possible. I am such a mess about adding binding on.

Make sure you get both the inner and outer layers of fleece sandwiched inside the binding.

Now it's time to work on assembling the 5 main pieces of the inner and outer portions of the guinea pig house.

Lay out your squares, putting them in the order you'd like them to be on your cube. You need three across, one above the center square and one below it.

Now you just sew each panel to the other, right sides together.

Now bear with me here. This part is tricky. You essentially need to sew the exterior fabrics into a cube (without a front panel, of course).

For example, the right side of the bottom blue square pictured above will be sewn right sides together with the bottom of the Doctor Who square that is above it to the right.

Then the left side of the blue square will be sewn right sides together to the Doctor Who square above it to the left.

Follow the same setup for the top blue square.

This creates an open cube (because we haven't sewn the front on yet).

REPEAT with the interior fabric pieces. This will give you two open cube pieces.

Here's a photo of the interior pieces, all sewn together.

At this point, you want to combine your interior and exterior pieces. Keep your interior fabrics as seen above.

Tuck your exterior fabric piece into it, right sides together and match up the edges. Pin.

Sew around the top, leaving an area to turn the whole thing right sides out. You want this gap to be a fist's width wide or so.

Turn right sides out!

When you turn it right sides out, it will look like this...

You need to tuck the inside back into the outside.

You'll need to add the front panel last. Flip your house so the interior fabrics are on the outside, then pin or clip your front panel to the opening, right sides together. Work around the whole thing, pinning carefully.

You'll see that I use those pretty red clips a lot. Those are special sewing clips that are a bit safer to use in the sewing room than pins. I find them faster for some types of projects. I use pins for some purposes still though.

Once pinned, you can use a straight stitch to sew the front panel on. You need to be VERY CAREFUL here. It requires sewing through a lot of layers and it's very easy to break a sewing needle. Using a larger size needle can help go through more layers, but I also choose to sew slowly around the corners where there's more bulk to the seam. That's usually where my machine has the most trouble. Change your needle out if you need to... needles dull with use.

When you're done, it should look like this next photo.

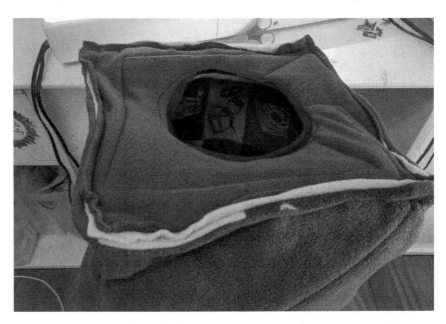

You just need to finish by pulling the whole thing through the entrance hole to the house.

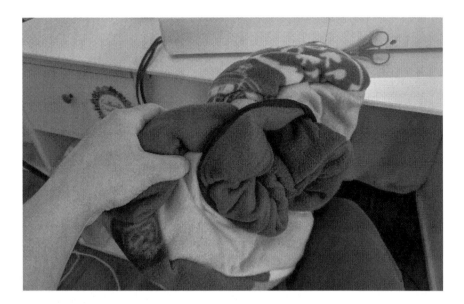

Thoughts on a better cube house:

I think I might quilt the outer fleece to the lining next time and leave the insides "free." This would allow me to easily pull the inside out through the front hole to clean the poops out. You can shake the poop out regardless, but I anticipate this might make for easier cleaning.

The first cube house that I made, pictured below, was super wonky. I used cotton for the exterior of it which I would not recommend. Fleece is far more forgiving for this project because it doesn't fray.

You can experiment with different types of stabilizer to create the stability in the sides of the house, but I liked that the batting offered stability while still keeping the product machine washable. This item will get peed and pooped in so you want to make sure you can wash it.

Hay Sack

When we got our guinea pigs, I got a metal hay rack, but I've since heard that they aren't a good idea because guinea pigs can get their heads stuck in them. I decided to try to make a hay bag instead. It's a great alternative as it holds lots of hay and it's washable. I like being able to throw it through the wash with our fleece cage liners.

Initially I thought that I'd made the opening in the front too big because the guinea pigs were able to get up into the bag, but this ended up being ideal. It hurts their necks to hold their heads up to eat (not a natural position for eating) and being able to crawl into the hay, play it in and eat is much better for them. I love happy mistakes.

Supplies

- Fleece fabric: 2 cuts that are 12x12"
- Grommets with <u>rings</u> or just use some fleece strips for ties

Instructions

You need to start by cutting two 12x12" pieces of fleece. Use whatever kind of fleece you would like. Prewash the fabric though to remove any chemicals.

You now need to take your front fabric and cut your squares. My finished square size was 3.5"x 3.5", but I'd start by cutting a 3.5x3.5" square, then cut the corners each at a diagonal like seen below. Initially I wanted a smaller hole so they COULDN'T get inside the bag, but now I wish I'd made the hole bigger because they love crawling inside and it's probably better for them than holding their neck up.

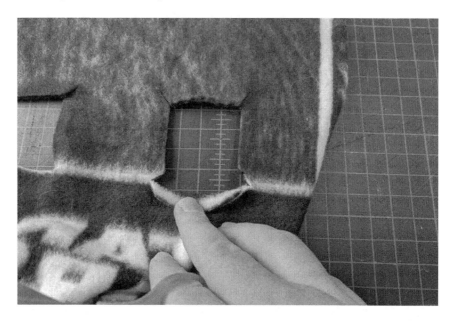

Now you can fold the fleece in for each side of the square and sew down with a straight stitch. It's not necessary (don't cut the diagonals if you don't want to do this) because fleece won't fray, but it just creates a more finished look.

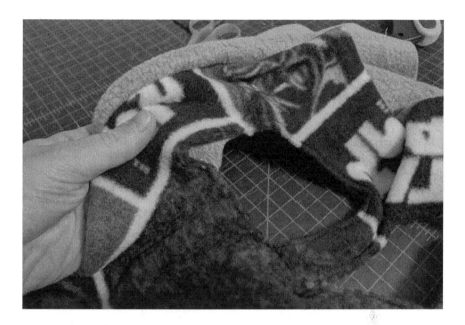

Now you need to sew your big pieces together. Face right sides together and sew along the bottom and two sides. Flip right sides out. Now you need to finish the top. Turn the top edge over and sew along it to create a finished look on the top.

I have a cheap grommet press that I got at the store and I hate it. It does the trick, but I haven't been impressed. I have been eyeballing the KX8J Handheld Press from Kam Snaps because it does grommets and snaps. Their stuff is high quality from what I've seen. I just haven't invested yet. You can use grommets like I did or just sew on some strips of fabric or other straps to tie the bag to the cage. I kind of like the idea of ties so I might try that for my next one.

I plan to make one or two more of these because I like to wash them... because the guinea pigs get into them, they collect hair and they get peed and pooped in. I usually launder the bag once a week and swap out with one of my other feeders.

Here it is finished and stuffed with hay.

Ball Toy

This project is a clever use for your scrap fleece. It's a small ball toy for the guinea pigs. I'm not sure if mine play with theirs, but I like the idea of it and it's a low effort project to try!

Supplies

- Fleece scraps

Instructions

You can start by taking scraps of fleece and cutting it into thin short strips.

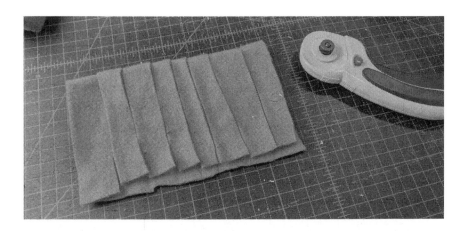

All you need to do is start with two strips and knot them together.

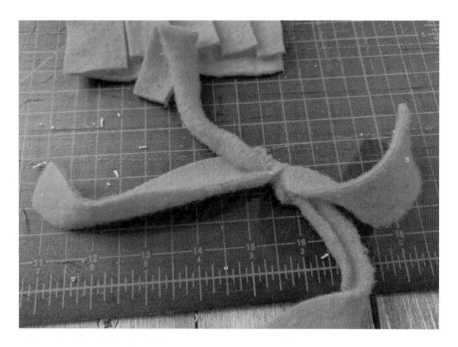

You can continue to knot new pieces around the center until you have a full ball shape.

If you want, you can use your scissors to trim the fleece to be a bit shorter.

Corner Hammock

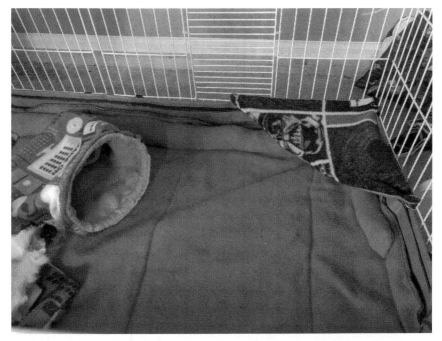

Many people like to create a corner hammock for their guinea pigs to sit on or snuggle under. This is an easy project to complete with scrap fleece. The one thing to note is that fleece tends to stretch... you may find you prefer a woven fabric if you don't want it to stretch as the guinea pigs stand on them.

Supplies

- Fleece or a woven fabric
- Grommets and Grommet Pliers (or you could make straps to tie on)

Instructions

You want to start by figuring out what size rectangle you want for your corner. If you take a piece of paper and cut it to fit into the corner, just as you would like your hammock to be, this is a great way to create a template- just make sure to add a ½" seam allowance to each side.

To make my hammocks, I cut two pieces of fabric each (I'm making two in the photos below). Then I faced the fabric right sides together and stitched around, leaving a space to turn the fabric right sides out.

You can now turn your fabric right sides out.

Top stitch your hammock.

At this point, you are done, and you can add a grommet to each of your corners. You'll use a binder ring, ribbon, or zip ties to attach the hammock to the corner of your cage.

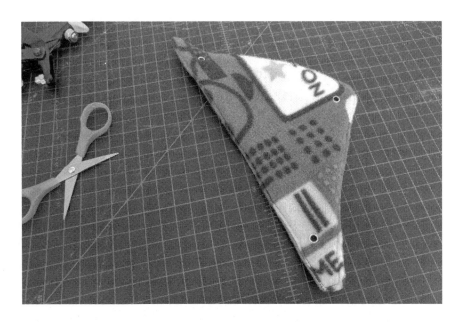

Alternative to Grommets: If you're intimidated by grommets, you could opt to use ties in each corner instead. Ribbon would work well. You would just add two strips of ribbon to each corner, sandwiched between your fabrics when you sew them right sides together. Then when you turn your fabric right sides out, your ribbons will pop out and be available for use. Tie around the rungs of your cage's corner.

Snuffle Mat

There's no sewing involved with this project, but it's fun and easy to make with your scrap fleece.

Supplies

- Fleece strips
- Sink mat

Instructions

The sink mat that I purchased was pretty large, so I started by cutting a square out of it. You can certainly use the entire thing, but it will take up a good part of your cage if you do. Make sure to trim off any sharp edges.

You'll want to start by cutting lots of strips of fabric. If you cut with the stretch going along the length of the strip, you'll find the strips pull and thin as you tie them. It's not a huge issue, but it's something to consider. I didn't notice the difference until I was tying the pieces on and some stretched more than others. Personally, I liked the ones that didn't stretch so I would plan for that if I made another.

A couple of notes on the size of your strips. I liked working with an 8" long x 1-1.5" wide strip. I found that gave me enough room to tie pieces on either side and that it was plenty long enough. I did, however, cut a variety of sizes. A few ended up being harder to tie because they were too short.

You can certainly do all your cutting with scissors, but I'm using a rotary blade with a straight edge quilting ruler in the photo. This made the work much faster and easier.

Here are some of my strips. I cut lots and lots of strips with different colors.

Once you cut the strips, you can just tie each one on.

I tied them on with a double knot. I tied a strip on every horizontal and every vertical bar.

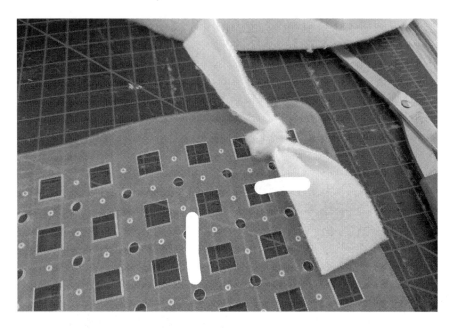

The back looked like this.

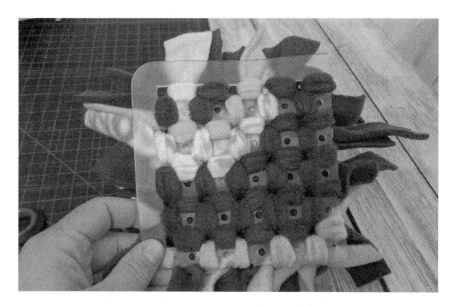

After you're done, just go and trim any extra long pieces.

This is a simple project and if you keep the size of your mat small, it should be fairly quick work. It's perfect to work on while watching tv.

Once you finish, you can put it in your pets' cage and add treats among the fabric.

Lap Blanket

If you plan to hold your guinea pigs a lot and are concerned about getting poop or pee on you, you may want to make a lap blanket to help protect your clothing. The idea with this is that you want something that is washable, somewhat waterproof and has absorbency. I added a pocket, but the pocket is optional.

Supplies

- Fleece
- Absorbency fabric such as an old towel (I used a cut of terrycloth)

Instructions

Cut your fabric. You need (2) cuts of fleece and (1) cut of terrycloth that are 11.5x21".

Optional Pocket

Cut a piece of fabric for the pocket that is 9.5x12.5".

Fold over the 9.5" side of your pocket fabric and sew it with a straight stitch. This will be the opening for your pocket.

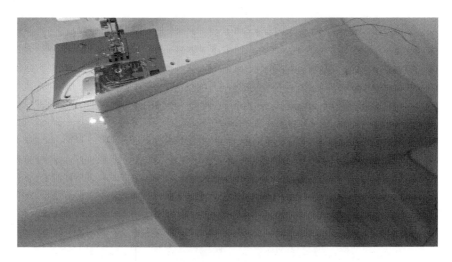

You need to fold over your other three edges as well, then pin it to your top fabric for the blanket.

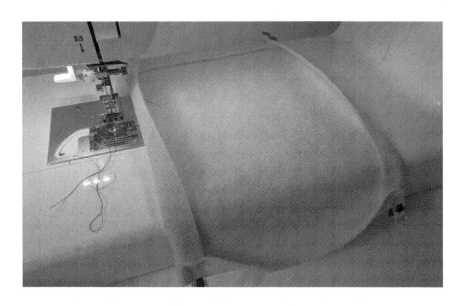

Sew around in a "U," leaving the front of the pocket open. I like to backstitch over the front of the pocket to reinforce the seam.

Now you can sew the regular part of your lap blanket.

Sewing the main lap blanket

To create your blanket, you need to layer your fabric with the terrycloth on the bottom, the bottom fleece right sides up on top, then the top fleece right sides down. Pin.

Sew around these three fabrics, making sure to catch all three. Leave a small area to turn and top stitch.

Turn. Topstitch. Normally I would iron before top stitching, but fleece doesn't iron well so I don't bother.

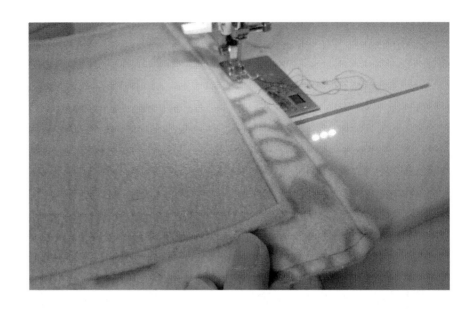

Ladder Cover

Wire cages and ladders aren't really kind to your guinea pig's feet, so you want to make something to cover them. The internal ladder for our cage had a cover, but not the ladder leading out of the cage. We use this ladder for them to play outside the cage, so I decided to whip up a quick and easy cover for the ladder.

I made two so you could see the difference between the stretch knit (fleece) and a woven (not stretchy) fabric. The nice thing about the stretch is that you have room for error because the fabric can stretch tight over the ladder. If you use fleece, it's also warm and not as prone to fraying.

You can make these two layers of fabric or even add

batting if you want to add thickness between the wire ladder and your guinea pig's feet.

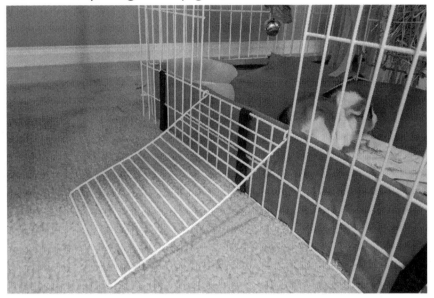

Supplies

- Fabric: The blue and white is fleece and the stripes are made from upholstery fabric.
- Optional: Batting, double layer of fabric

I want to mention that this could be made for any ramp, but the ramp that I made this one for is the exterior "door" in the Midwest Guinea Pig Habitat cage. As mentioned previously, the cage includes an inner ramp that is double sided and comes with a ramp cover that is 18.5 x 7. Unfortunately, they don't seem to offer ramp covers for the outside wire doors that come down and we let our guinea pigs out using those ramps. I made these to cover the wire to protect their feet from getting caught or injured on the wire. I'll talk about how to get your own measurements for your cage, but I'll using my measurements for this cage.

Instructions

You need to start by measuring your ladder. You will need the width and length of your ladder.

Once you have those measurements, you need to add a seam allowance on. Most people add a ¼" or ½" seam allowance, but you need to add this measurement to all sides. For example, if you have a 9.25" x 7" ladder, then a ¼" added seam allowance means you add a ½" to each side to equal 9.75" x 7.5". If I had preferred a ½" seam allowance, then I'd be adding 1" to each dimension to equal 10.25" x 8".

Now you need to add extra length to account for the amount that will overlap. I used around a 3" overlap.

For my Midwest exterior ramp, I cut my fabric at 12.75" x 7.5".

This is a pretty simple project that only took 5 minutes once I figured out the measurements.

I turned over the edges of each long edge and sewed them down using a straight stitch. If you're using a fabric that is prone to fraying, you'll want to either do a double fold or zig zag/serge the edges (if you do this, you'll need to add extra seam allowance).

The amount you turn your edge over is your seam allowance. If you used a ¼" seam allowance, then you want to turn over each edge ¼".

Do this to both long sides, then do it to both of your short sides.

To finish, you fold over the bottom part of your ramp so it is wrong sides together with the rest of the fabric with a 3" overlap. This will be the section that slides over the ramp bottom to hold it snuggly on. It allows you to remove it easily, as well, for cleaning.

Sew a straight stitch on both sides to hold the overlap down.

I was wishing I'd made it a bit longer, but it was pretty stretchy so it worked out okay. I made the woven version longer as a result.

Here are a few pictures of the woven version. The process was exactly the same, except I serged the edges because my fabric was fraying (that's the fancy stitching).

If you want to add a double layer of fabric or add batting, I'll explain briefly how to do this.

Cut two pieces of fabric that are 12.75" x 7.5". Your batting would be the same size (or slightly smaller if you want to avoid bulk around the edges) as well, if you're using it. Quilt the batting to one of the fabric pieces.

Now face the two pieces of fabric right sides together. Sew around, leaving a small space to turn.

Turn right sides out. Top stitch.

Fold over your extra 3" and sew down to create the pocket that holds the cover on the ramp.

Conclusion

Are your guinea pigs spoiled enough yet? Make them matching sets that you can swap out whenever you want. Fleece is affordable and goes on sale frequently… it would be fun to have holiday sets!

We love our fleece. It's so soft and it washes well. The guinea pigs always look super snuggly in their cage.

Make sure to keep an eye out for other pet and guinea pig projects on diydanielle.com.

You can see the supply and resource list for this book at https://diydanielle.com/sewing-guinea-pigs/supplies-sewing-guineapigs/

Glossary

Absorbency Fabric: The absorbency layer of fabric is the fabric that will absorb and hold liquid in it. A good example of this is the fabric towels are made from. When you dry off with your towel after a shower, the moisture sits in the towel and doesn't drip onto the floor. Some fabrics have more or less absorbency to them, and some absorb faster or slower. Often there is a tradeoff... for example, some fabrics absorb very slow but hold a lot of liquid.

Casing: A casing is generally used to enclose an elastic or draw string. It's a narrow channel that is sewn wide enough to accommodate the width of the elastic, draw string, or other item. The use of the casing allows you to avoid sewing an elastic into the fabric.

Polyurethane Laminate (PUL): A fabric type that was originally made for hospital use because it could be washed and dried on hot heat. This fabric has become more common over the past 10 years as it is used in modern cloth diapers.

Right Side of the Fabric: The "right" side is the side you want facing out when you're finished.

Seam Allowance: The extra fabric you cut out for your pattern that accounts for the overlap of fabric when you're sewing. This seam allowance will generally be hidden from view. If you look at the interior of your shirt, for example, you can see where the seamstress sewed together the pieces (usually at the sides).

Stay Dry Fabric: This term refers to fabrics that wick moisture through the fabric rather than letting moisture pool on top of it. Once it absorbs through the fabric into an absorbency layer below, the stay dry fabric should feel dry to the touch unless the absorbency is completely soaked.

Top Stitch: This references the stitch you use as a finishing stitch that shows up on your finished product. People will be able to see this stitch, so you want to choose a thread color that is attractive or that blends in with your fabric.

Wicking Fabric vs. Non-Wicking Fabric: A wicking fabric will take moisture and wick it into an absorbency liner underneath. Some fleece wicks and some doesn't, but you need to prep your fleece before you can determine if it will truly wick. The problem is that chemicals used on fabric can prevent wicking initially, so you'll need to prewash to get them off. You cannot use fabric softener or detergent with fabric softener on your cloth products as those will add those chemicals right back in.

Here is an example of wicking vs. non-wicking. Both fabrics have been prewashed and are fleece.

Photo 1: When a few drops of water are dripped on this fleece, the water sits on top. It may eventually soak through, but it takes quite some time. This is a non-wicking fabric.

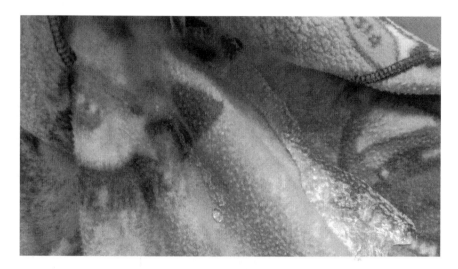

Photo 2: When a few drops of water are dripped on this fleece, the water goes right through. It's quick. It can only work so fast though so when you're testing, don't pour a gallon of water on. You need to put 2-5 drops on top of the fabric.

I think there's supposed to be types of fleece that wick or don't wick, but I always test. I don't think I've ever gotten decorative fleece that wicks well.

Woven Fabric: Woven fabrics do not stretch due to how the fabric is made (it is made by weaving threads together… check out YouTube if you want to see some cool videos of this in action). Woven fabric generally frays around the edges unless the edges are finished.

Wrong Side of the Fabric: The wrong side of the fabric is the side that isn't meant to be seen. The ugly side, so to speak. Some fabrics, however, don't have a wrong side or the wrong side isn't easily identified.

About the Author

Danielle Pientka lives in Maryland with her three sons, her husband, and her pets. She writes about sewing, woodworking, crafts, and gardening on her DIY blog, diydanielle.com. She loves spending time outdoors and creating things from scratch. She is always on a mission to learn new things.

Other Books by Danielle Pientka

14 Simple Sewing Projects for Your Kitchen: This book focuses on sewing projects that you can complete for your kitchen.

How to Sew, Use, and Clean Cloth Diapers: This book teaches you all about cloth diapers, as well as about other reusable cloth products like unpaper towels, cloth menstrual pads, and more.

A Month to Happiness Journal: A Guided Journal with Prompts to Help Focus on Positive Aspects of Your Life

Thanks for reading! As a self-published author, I rely on reviews from my readers. Please take time to write a review on Amazon or Goodreads.

Made in the USA
Columbia, SC
09 June 2022

61541924R00052